Dynamite's Funny Book of the Sad Facts of Life

by Jovial Bob Stine

Illustration by Jared Lee

A Dynamite Book from Scholastic Paperbacks

The Book You Are Holding Is 100% Dynamite!

Yes, Dynamite Books come to you from the same
scintillating scribblers and peerless pen and inkers who
bring you *Dynamite* magazine every month: Jane Stine,
Editorial Director; Greg Wozney Design, Art Direction;
Sharon Graham, Production Editor; Susan Hood,
Assistant Editor, plus the whole Hot Stuff gang!

ISBN: 0-590-30620-0

12 11 10 9 8 7 6 5 4 3 2 1   5   0 1 2 3 4 5/8

Printed in the U.S.A.   11

Important Reminder Page

Why is it that every time you find a few free minutes and settle down in a quiet corner to start reading a new book, someone calls you to do some chore you were supposed to do? So you put the book down and go do the chore, and when you get back, you can't find your place, and besides it's time for supper!

Why is it? Well, it's just one of the Sad Facts of Life. But since this is a funny book about all the Sad Facts of Life, we've done something about this one! We've given you this . . .

IMPORTANT REMINDER PAGE!

Our Important Reminder is: Go do that chore. Go see why they're calling you. We'll wait right here for you. We won't go on with the book until you get back. Promise!

Well . . . go on, get going! Don't just sit there! This is our last reminder before the book gets started. . . .

TABLE OF CONTENTS

INTRODUCTION

It's one of the Sad Facts of Life
that nobody ever reads Introductions.
So we didn't write one.

Help! Please Help! You Must Save Me! You Must!!

Some books will do anything to get your attention.

First, they leave out the Introduction. Then they throw in a page with a scary, dramatic headline that has nothing to do with the book!

We know you're too smart to be fooled by anything like that. So we wouldn't even try it.

Honest.

CONGRATULATIONS!
You Are Our Lucky Grand-Prize Winner!!

And while you're waiting to find out what your Grand Prize will be, we'll try to explain what this book is all about.

You see, we'd like to show how all the terrible little things that happen in life can actually be funny, and to demonstrate that if you go through life with a smile, you . . . uh . . . well . . . . Uh-oh.

You caught us, didn't you?!

You caught us trying to trick you into reading an Introduction. The fact is, you're not our Grand-Prize Winner after all.

Sorry about that. But we've learned our lesson. We won't try to slip anything else past you.

Let's get this funny, sad book started. No more Introductions. Onward!

When should you start worrying about the Sad Facts of Life? Well, there's no time like the present. Even while you're beginning this fabulous book, you may have big troubles! For example, here are ...

8 Things To Worry About While You're Reading This Book

---

1. Your friends are all reading it, and they might give away the exciting ending.

2. You might laugh too hard and fall off a mountain.

3. You might be allergic to silly lists.

4. You might accidentally close your finger between the pages and not be able to get it out.

5. Why doesn't the book have an Introduction?

6. The book might have you in stitches — and you don't have time to get the stitches removed.

7. You may accidentally be holding it upside down, and it won't make any sense at all to you.

8. You may be holding it right-side up, and it *still* won't make any sense to you!

It's a Sad Fact of Life that even the happiest occasions have their trying moments. Take that birthday party you've been invited to. Sure, you're probably going to have a great time. But before you start gulping down the birthday cake and playing Pin the Tail on the Host, you might want to think about these . . .

20 Sad Facts About Birthday Parties!

1. The birthday cake won't taste half as good as it looks. (And there'll be candle wax stuck to the piece you get.)

2. No one will really want to play all those silly games, but no one will be brave enough to refuse.

3. Mark and Ann-Marie won't really be kissing in the hall, but they'll want everyone to think they were.

4. None of the boys will want to dance, and girls will have to dance with girls again.

5. There's only ginger ale in the punch, but some kids will stagger around and act crazy from it. (Only two or three people will think they're funny, and you won't be one of them.)

6. Someone will spill Coke on the couch and cover it up by turning the cushion around.

7. The guests will break most of the birthday kid's presents before they leave.

8. Some people will talk about how last week's party was better than this one. (You weren't invited to last week's.)

9. If you get all dressed up, everyone will wear jeans. If you wear jeans, everyone else will be dressed up!

10. They'll run out of hot-dog rolls when they get to you, and you'll have to eat yours on bread. (You'll still manage to drip mustard all over your shirt.)

11. The birthday kid's father will take hours getting everyone posed so he can take a picture, and then the flashbulb won't work.

12. No matter how many times you tell your father the correct time, he'll still arrive an hour early to pick you up. (He'll stay and have some cake and ice cream and say a lot of things that will embarrass you.)

13. The rope will tear during the tug-of-war and two kids will need bandages on their hands for rope burn. One kid will cut his lip on a plastic drinking cup. One will laugh while drinking and send soda pop through his nose. Two kids will get hiccups that last all afternoon. (You'll be one of them.)

14. Someone will try to cheat during Pin-the-Tail, but he'll be discovered and the blindfold will be made tighter for everyone.

15. You'll try to be polite to the birthday kid's parents, but you'll forget their names. (They won't remember yours, either. For some reason, they'll call you Donny all afternoon even though there's no one at the party named Donny. After a while, you'll get tired of correcting them.)

16. You'll win a really stupid door prize and throw it away before you get home.

17. The elderly neighbor lady from next door will drop in to "see how cute everyone looks" and she'll trip over a roller skate and be hit in the head with a flying hot-dog roll.

18. The neighbors on the other side will ask you to turn down the record player, but you won't be able to hear them because the record player is so loud.

19. The birthday kid's mother will be upset when she finds potato-chip dip in the cuckoo clock. (Wait till she finds what someone put in the geraniums!)

20. You *really will* be sorry you ate that third piece of cake and fourth helping of caramel raspberry chocolate almond ice cream with butterscotch sauce!

The Sad Facts About the Weather

What's the weather going to be tomorrow — sunny and hot or rainy and cool? You say you can't predict the weather? Of course you can! That's because the Sad Fact about the weather is that it's more predictable than you think.

You can test your weather-predicting abilities by checking over this predictably ridiculous checklist. Just circle your prediction for each situation, and you'll start to see how easy it is to be an accurate forecaster. (Don't forget your umbrella!)

1. Your class has been planning an all-day picnic in a nearby woods for six months. Everyone brings a picnic basket full of food, and lots of outdoor sports are planned. The class takes a bus to the woods. As you step out of the bus, the weather is:
   a) rain
   b) rain
   c) rain
   d) rain with occasional rain

2. You have been home sick in bed for three days. Every time you gather up enough strength to look out the window, you see that it is bright and sunny outside. Finally, Saturday rolls around and you are well enough to go outside.

As you open the front door, the weather is:
  a) heavy rain
  b) heavy rain with periods of rain
  c) rain (not to mention rain)
  d) more rain (hey, didn't we say not to mention rain?)

3. Your Little League team has had an embarrassing season. You lost your most recent game by 32 runs — and that was your best game of the season. The final game of the year is scheduled for Tuesday, and it's with the toughest team in the league. You'd do anything to get out of playing that game. You pray and pray for rain so you won't have to play the game and be embarrassed again. On Tuesday the weather is:
  a) sunny and mild
  b) sunny and warm
  c) sunny and bright
  d) sunny and fair

4. You are all dressed up in your best outfit to go to a party. Just before you leave, your mother says it might rain. She makes you put on your raincoat, your galoshes, and your rain hat, and she makes you carry an umbrella. As you walk to the party (and for the rest of the day) the weather is:

a) sunny and mild
b) sunny with sun
c) sunny with patches of sun
d) sunny and even sunnier with occasional sun

5. You've worked for six weeks to build a float for the Fourth of July parade. In addition to a map of your state made entirely from gladiolas and carnations, your float contains two complete marching bands and the school choir. It has to be the best float ever built, and you can't wait for the crowds along the parade route to see it. As the parade begins on the morning of July 4, the weather is:

a) raining buckets
b) raining cats and dogs
c) raining very large cats and dogs
d) raining buckets of cats and dogs

6. On the night before the disastrous Fourth of July parade, the weather forecaster on TV predicted:

a) sunny and mild
b) sunny and warm
c) sunny and hot
d) partly cloudy

**Is it possible that adorable,
quiet little puppy will grow into a howling,
six-foot-tall, hungry beast before he's six
months old? Of course not! But before you carry
that cuddly creature home from the pet store,
maybe you'd better consider these....**

Sad Facts About Pets!

You'll spend two weeks building your dog a comfortable dog bed in the cellar, and when it's all finished, he'll sleep on the floor next to it!

No matter how much you oil it, your hamster's exercise wheel will still squeak and keep you up all night!

Your cat will develop clever ways of letting you know when she's tired of being petted. Better keep the Band-Aids handy.

Your cat and dog will get along perfectly — except when you're bragging about them in front of company. That's when they'll decide to re-stage the heavyweight championship fight!

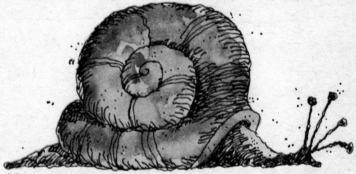

No matter how many snails you put in to "eat up the dirt," your fish tank will be dirty again 10 minutes after you clean it!

In two months that adorable little puppy who cowers and shakes whenever anyone comes near will be five feet tall, weigh 250 pounds, and will constantly get you in trouble by picking up passersby and burying them in the backyard!

Your canary sings beautifully and endless-ly — until you walk over to listen to it!

By the time you buy the fancy aquarium, the electric filters, and all the other equipment, you won't be able to afford to buy any fish!

No matter what kind of cage or container you put him in, that little turtle you won at the carnival will climb out and disappear the first chance it gets, and you'll never see him again.

Your cat only likes to rub up against your legs when you're in a hurry and trying to get somewhere really fast.

All the books say that a parakeet will get quiet as soon as you cover its cage — but you'll find out your parakeet obviously hasn't read the books!

Petting a snake can get pretty boring after a few minutes.

You can look for your cat for hours when you want to play with her and never find her. Then when you're busy and have all kinds of important things to do, she'll want to walk across your face.

Gerbils will not come when they hear their names called. It isn't too easy to teach them to roll over, either.

As much as you promise yourself you won't do it, you'll never be able to resist giving your dog all the table scraps he wants.

The "family pet" will always be referred to as "your pet" whenever it does anything bad!

Baseball Puzzlers
Some Questions We've Never Been Able To Answer!

1. After a batter swings and misses and strikes out, why does he always look at his bat?

2. Why do they always pull the pitcher out of the game *after* he's given up six runs instead of *before*?

3. Why aren't there any tall shortstops?

4. Why does your favorite player always hit a home run when you've just gone out for a hot dog?

5. Why does your team lose every game that's on TV and win all the games you can't see?

**All these Sad Facts beginning to get you down?
Well, cheer up —there are plenty more to come!
But if you insist, let's take a break for some
good news....**

Why It's Great To Have Brothers and Sisters

You're not the only one who won't eat the lima beans.

There are more birthdays to celebrate — and more presents that your brothers and sisters will be delighted to share with you!

When your older brother goes away for the weekend, you can listen to his great record collection, and he won't mind a bit — unless he finds out!

There are always interesting phone conversations to listen to and pretend you're not listening to them!

Your room is only one of *several* in the house that looks as if it was in the path of Hurricane Harry!

There's always someone around to fight with so you don't have to fight with your friends.

There's always someone else who would rather watch *The Brady Bunch* instead of the news — so your father is out-voted again at the TV set!

You're not the only one who won't eat the liver!

You get to share your clothes, which means you don't have to spend a lot of time shopping and wearing itchy new clothes.

You have someone to practice the new dance steps with so you don't make too big a fool of yourself in public!

You're not the only one who won't eat the cauliflower!

There's always someone around who can keep a secret from your mother — at least until she gets home from the store!

And now for those of you who are the only kid in the family, let's drop the Sad Facts for a while and take a look at the good news for you. . . .

Why It's Great To Be the Only Kid

That whole birthday cake is for you!

There's no one around to break your toys before you get a chance to!

When your parents get angry, you don't have to try to figure out who they're yelling about!

You don't have to worry about wearing out your clothes because there's no one you have to pass them on to!

There's room enough to lie down in the back seat of the car during those long, boring car trips in which your mother points out every cow and horse!

When you're sick, no one else will complain that they caught what you have!

No one ever asks, "Why can't you behave like your brother?" or "Why can't you get good grades like your sister?"

You don't have to fight over who's going to take

the first bath and who's going to take the last bath!

You never have to share a stick of gum.

No one ever calls you by the wrong name.

You don't have to hunt for hours through the family album to find a photo of yourself. There are dozens of embarrassing ones on every page!

Sometimes you know it's you that's talking — but you can't believe the words that are coming out of your mouth! You know it's too late, but you just want to scream . . .

Why Did I Say That?!!

"If you two want to go out tonight, Mom and Dad, I'll stay home and take care of Little Billy."

"Sure, you're more than welcome to join the guys and me throwing the football around, Dad!"

"Yeah, I'll defend you against those bullies that are picking on you. What are friends for?"

"I can work that algebra problem out on the chalkboard, Miss Grimmly. It's a snap!"

"No, Mom, it wouldn't embarrass me if you came to school to watch me give my science report."

"I'll get that angry dog off the playground. I know how to handle animals!"

"Your bike is broken and you can't enter the 50-mile bike race? Why don't you borrow mine?"

"Pass the hot peppers. Nothing is too spicy for me!"

"If you'll give me an advance on my allowance, I'll put three-fourths of it away for college."

"I'm not feeling too well. Do you think I should skip school today, Mom, so I can go to the party tonight?"

"I'll untie that knot for you in a jiffy. You won't believe how good I am at untying knots!"

"So you think you're on a high limb? You don't know anything about climbing trees. I can climb clear to the top. Dare me?"

"You're worried because Grandma is coming to visit for a month? Why don't you give her my room so she'll be more comfortable?"

It's a Sad Fact of School Life that things are quite different on test days. The halls are quieter. The clocks are noisier. And then there are these other ...

Sad Facts of Taking Tests

If you bring four or five sharpened pencils, you use only one for the whole test. If you bring only one pencil, it breaks while you're writing your name at the top of the page!

If you memorized every fact in Chapter Four, the test is almost entirely about Chapter Three.

The teacher always seems to smile more on test days!

It's always quiet outside your classroom window. Then the moment you start to take a test, a fight breaks out, sirens go off, people scream, and horns honk!

You think you've answered Number Four correctly with just five words. But the kid next to you has written five paragraphs and is still going!

There's always one student in the class who puts down his or her pencil and asks the teacher, "What should I do now? I'm finished!" when you're still on Question Three.

Someone makes the clock go twice as fast as it normally does.

The kid next to you who copies every single answer off your paper gets a higher score than you do.

The teacher tells the class, "Don't mark on the test. Use an answer sheet," after you've filled in the entire test!

The test is still wet, and now you've got purple ditto ink all over your clothes.

The empty seats in your classroom seem to indicate that the 24-hour virus strikes more often on test days then any other time of the year!

Someone always comes in to talk to your teacher during the test, and you can't help but concentrate more on what they're saying than on your answers.

You finish with a little time to spare, so you go back and change a few of your answers. Later, you find out that all the answers were right the first time.

You know the material so well, you're positive you're getting every answer right. And the teacher announces, "Today's test doesn't count. It's just a practice exam for the real test tomorrow."

Just as the bell rings and you start to pass the papers to your teacher, you remember the correct answers to Questions Five, Seven, Eight, and Twelve!

Doctor Puzzlers
Some Questions We've Never Been Able To Answer!

---

1. Do doctors really keep their stethoscopes in the freezer, or do they just feel that way?

2. Why can't you say "ohhhh" instead of "aaaaaaaah"?

3. Why does the doctor always tell you to breathe normally when you're already breathing normally?

4. Why do doctors ask, "How are you feeling?" when they *know* you're sick?

5. Why do doctors always say, "This won't hurt," just before they hurt you?

The Sad Facts About Relatives

One funny Sad Fact about relatives is that we all seem to have the same ones. Sure, they go by different names. Your family may have an Aunt Millie while the family across the street has an Aunt Molly. But, put them in a room with a bunch of nieces and nephews, and they'll act exactly the same.

You want proof? Okay, check out this relatively simple Relative Checklist. How many of these relatives are related to you? Put an X next to the ones you have in your family!

_____ **AUNT MOLLY. The Pincher.**
Her thumb and first finger are bigger than the rest of her hand because she likes to pinch so

much. She pinches your cheek when she arrives for a visit. Then she gives your arm a pinch when you bring her a piece of fruit. Sometimes she pinches you for no reason at all.

_____ **UNCLE NEDDY. The Hugger.**
He's married to The Pincher. Insists on having a big hug every time he arrives or leaves. Gives you a present and then demands another big hug. Too bad he doesn't know his own strength. Your ribs ache for days afterward.

_____ AUNT LUCY. The Speller.

Always spells out words when you're in the room. She doesn't want your young ears to hear anything naughty. She doesn't know what a good speller you are. Sometimes you even have to correct her spelling!

_____ UNCLE MURRAY. The Joker.

Thinks he's really a funny guy. Always drags you in a corner to tell you 20 or 30 jokes. You've heard them all before, but you laugh anyway. He tells everyone, "Kids really like me because I speak their language."

_____ AUNT ALICE. The Talent Scout.

Always begs to see you perform. "Come on, dance for us. Come on, sing a song for your aunt. Play your guitar for us." Always embarrasses you in front of a roomful of relatives.

____ UNCLE WILLY. The Height Inspector.

Tells you how tall you're getting every time you walk into the room. Thinks you're terribly talented just because you grow. Insists on dragging you into the kitchen and making a mark on the wall to show your height. Your mother makes you wash the mark off as soon as he leaves.

____ GRANDMA WILLA. The Gift-Giver.

Brings you terrible gifts every time she visits. Can't wait for you to open them. The clothes are always too small. The toys are always too babyish. After she leaves, you have to write her a thank-you note, even though you'll never look at the present again.

____ GRANDPA IKE. The Fan.

Thinks everything you say and do is clever and brilliant. Always repeats every word you say to the entire room. "Didja hear what the kid just said? He said he'd like some root beer! Ha ha! Do you believe it? What a mouth! Hey, look how he shakes hands! Whatta kid!"

____ UNCLE MIKE. The Smoker.

Always forces you to take a puff on his cigar. Says, "Go ahead, it'll make you a man." Then yells to everyone, "Hey look — the kid's smoking cigars now! Haw Haw Haw!" Thinks it's a riot when you start to cough and choke.

____ AUNT BARBARA. The Bad Sport.

She's married to Uncle Mike. She always has to say, "Mike, leave the kid alone. Can't you see he doesn't want your cigar?" Then she and Uncle Mike get into a big fight. You're left standing in the middle, holding the cigar and getting sick while they battle it out.

____ AUNT MINNIE. The Spoiler.

Always slipping you more sweets and dessert than your parents want you to have. Makes you eat a whole box of candy even though you don't want it. Then when you're exhausted from all the food she's stuffed you with, she tells your parents, "Aw, come on. Let him stay up an extra hour. What's it going to hurt?"

___ UNCLE JACK. The Athlete.

Forces you to go out in the backyard and throw a ball around with him. Won't listen when you say you have homework to do. Tries to show off but always drops the ball. Throws the ball way into the next lot and then makes you chase it.

___ UNCLE NATE. The Businessman.

Always wants to know what you want to be when you grow up. Asks every time he sees you. Can't believe you haven't decided yet. Always ends up by advising you to go into thermoplastics. That's because he's in thermoplastics.

___ UNCLE BERT. The Magician.

Calls you over to do magic tricks for you every time he visits. Likes to make a quarter appear from your ear or pull an egg from your pocket. Always makes you feel like a fool. Keeps refusing to tell you how the tricks are done, even though you already guessed years ago.

___ AUNT HELEN. The Name-Caller.

She's the last of your relatives who still calls you by your baby nickname. All the other aunts and uncles know that you hate it, but she insists on calling you "Boo Boo" every time she sees you — usually in front of all of your friends!

Every day should start with a good breakfast. But sadly, some days start with the kind of breakfast that could send you back to bed — for a week! What do we mean? Well ...

You Know You Should Have Skipped Breakfast When:

Your cornflakes are limp and soggy *before* you pour the milk on!

You can't decide which side of the toast to butter!

Instead of "Snap! Crackle! Pop!" your cereal says, "Help! Help! Help!"

One of your fried eggs winks at you!

There wasn't time to thaw the frozen orange juice, so your mother gives it to you on a stick!

You accidentally put salt in your cereal and sugar on your eggs.

You've reminded yourself a thousand times to let the hot chocolate cool before you burn your tongue off, but it seems you need one thousand and *one* reminders!

Your alphabet cereal spells out: WARNING: CAN BE HAZARDOUS TO YOUR HEALTH.

The raisins in your cereal fly away.

That was chili sauce — not cherry preserves — you spread on your pancakes!

Someone forgot to hard-boil the egg you just cracked over your lap!

Lost & Found Department

It's a Sad Fact of Life that most books don't have a Lost & Found Department. Well, a lot of people lose things and find things all the time. And we say, so what if we are right in the middle of a book? If people need a Lost & Found Department, we're going to give them one — right now. . . .

LOST! The alligator is missing from my alligator shirt. I refuse to be seen in an alligator shirt if the alligator is missing. Reward if found. (The shirt is missing too, and it's freezing in here. Please hurry.) Allan.

LOST! I lost my voice during choir practice last Tuesday. I found it a few hours later, but it was too late to do any singing. I don't know why I'm telling you about it. I guess I just wanted to be in a book. Susan.

FOUND! One 800-pound St. Bernard who eats like a horse and smells like one, too. Won't stop drooling. (The dog won't stop — not me.) Don't get confused. I'm very confused because the dog has taken over my room and I've been sleeping out in the rain. Owner may come get dog any time. Bill.

LOST! One 800-pound St. Bernard who eats like a horse and smells like one, too. I'm sorry to hear about your room, Bill, but you're stuck with the dog. I'm never coming to pick him up. Sorry. Former Dog Owner.

FOUND! One copy of *Dynamite's Funny Book of the Sad Facts of Life!* Someone seems to have started the Lost & Found chapter and then thrown the book away. I can't say that I blame them. What's a Lost & Found Department doing in a book anyway? I guess I'll keep the book. I don't think anyone else would want it. Name Withheld.

LOST! I lost my courage when I was just about to ask Mary Ann for a date. Can anyone help me find it? Can anyone help me find Mary Ann? I haven't seen her in ages. Maybe I don't know anyone named Mary Ann. I guess I don't need any help after all. Thanks anyway. Confused.

LOST! All of my school supplies are missing. I had them in my locker and now they're gone. Here's what's missing: one red number-2 pencil, one yellow number-2 pencil, one number-3 pencil with eraser, one blue ballpoint pen, one green soft-tip pen, one fountain pen, one bottle of blue-black ink, one yellow tablet with wide rules, one white tablet with narrow rules, one stenographer's notepad with spiral binding, one looseleaf notebook with three rings, one looseleaf — oh, wait a minute. Oh, wait. Here's my stuff over here. Gee, I was looking in the wrong locker. My stuff is all here in my locker. Wayne.

FOUND! One 800-pound St. Bernard who — oh — have I already mentioned this? Sorry. Bill.

LOST! One hot-air balloon. A gust of wind carried it away from its moorings. Now the balloon is 10,000 feet in the air and floating over unidentified territory. I wouldn't mind so much — except I'm in it! Help! Help! Somebody! Get me down! Help me! Help! HellllllllP! Worried.

FOUND! One thingamajig. It's attached to a whatsis. I believe it must have come loose from a thingamabob. If it's yours, you can carry it away if you bring the right doohicky. Alice.

FOUND! An empty brown paper bag. I found it by the side of the road. If you can identify it, describe it, tell me what shape and color it is and how big it is and which side has the opening, and prove to me satisfactorily that it is yours, and bring three pieces of identification, and bring me a brown paper bag to replace it, I will gladly return it to you. Edith.

LOST! I seem to have lost my place in this book. Can anyone tell me where I left off? Or should I

I'M WATCHING EVERY MOVE YOU MAKE.

just start all over again at the Important Reminder Page? Uh-oh. Someone's calling me to milk the goat. Gee, I wish I didn't have to milk the goat. Especially since our goat is so ticklish. Know what I mean? Herman.

FOUND! Please come claim an ice cream cone I just found on this outdoor table. It's vanilla flavored and — wait a minute — I'd better taste it. No, it's not vanilla. It's sort of lemony and — wait — I'll just take one more bite. Hey, this is good! Get away — I'm finishing this! Go away! I don't care who you are! Finders keepers! You can't prove it's yours! Stop it! Don't grab! Okay, okay, I'll share it with you! Hey! Ouch! Freddy.

LOST! I've lost my sheep and don't know where to find them. Maybe I'll leave them alone and they'll come home, wagging their tails behind them. If they do, I'll have their hides removed, sell the wool at a profit, and live on lambchops all winter. It's a living. Bo Peep.

LOST! I've lost the will to go on reading these ridiculous Lost & Found items. Unless this chapter ends immediately, I will be forced to report you to the Martians who have landed in my backyard and are watching our every move. Please — pretend that everything is normal. Maybe they will go away. Just get on with the book. I don't want to involve them in this, but I will if I have to. Desperate To Move On To Another Chapter.

We interrupt Dynamite's Funny Book of the
Sad Facts of Life to
bring you this important Public
Service Feature. . . .

Excuses That Will Never Work In Any Class!

"I'd love to work that problem out on the chalkboard, but I'll wait till you have one that's a little more challenging."

"I *was* paying attention, Miss Bimmins. I just closed my eyes and put my head down on the desk so I could visualize what you were saying more clearly."

"I *did* my homework. But it was so good, I was afraid you'd think I copied it from somebody. So I'm doing it over."

"I wasn't absent yesterday. I was just a day tardy."

"No, I don't have a doctor's excuse — but I really *do* have an allergic reaction to handling books of any kind."

"I wasn't copying her answers. I was checking to make sure the blue rules on my paper were the same thickness as hers."

"I didn't lose my textbook. Somebody offered me $500 for it. I couldn't turn *that* down, could I?"

"I brought two pencils with me for the test. But the termites ate them before the bell rang."

"I wasn't whispering. I was silently mouthing the words to 'America, the Beautiful.' I do that from time to time when I'm really enjoying a class."

15 Things To Worry About When You're Buying an Ice Cream Cone

1. Maybe the cone costs 10 cents more than you have.

2. You might not get the flavor you asked for, and since you already took a bite out of it, you can't return it.

3. The first bite may be too cold and make your teeth hurt.

4. Maybe the cone wasn't packed tightly enough and the ice cream will fall out and plop onto your shoes.

5. The cone might crack in your hands and the ice cream will fall out and plop onto your shoes.

6. Maybe they'll give you a regular cone when you asked for a sugar cone.

7. Maybe you'll get tired of it after a few bites, and there won't be any place to throw it away.

8. Maybe you asked for Almond Fudge Ripple Caramel Berry Whip Tutti Frutti Surprise when you really meant to ask for Almond Fudge Ripple Caramel Berry Whip Tutti Frutti Delight!

9. You might get a spot of ice cream on your nose and your friends won't tell you.

10. Maybe your friend who ordered the same size cone as you got a bigger scoop of ice cream than you did.

11. Maybe there's a hole in the bottom of the cone and all the ice cream will drip onto your new shirt.

12. Maybe your tongue will freeze after a few bites and you won't be able to taste the rest of the ice cream.

13. Maybe a big dog will come along and force you to share your cone with him.

14. Maybe you'll get it all over your face and hands and not be able to find a napkin.

15. Maybe you really wanted a sundae instead of a cone.

Sure, you're very popular and make friends easily, but it's a Sad Fact of Life that sometimes you've got to be a little choosy. What do we mean? Well, our advice is that ...

It's Best To Stay Away From a Kid Who ...

rides to school on the back of another kid!

has hands that drag along the sidewalk as he walks, a hairy chest, and a crush on Fay Wray!

sucks down a dozen raw eggs right from the shell for lunch every day.

likes to cut the front lawn with his teeth!

invites you to a Chipmunk Squeezing Party.

tells you she flies home to the planet Jupiter every night.

asks you to help her with her witchcraft homework!

has a rubber-tree plant growing out of his forehead!

likes to spray-paint his initials on the backs of people who walk by.

tries to sell you a ticket to the cockroach races!

wears a black cape, has long, pointy fangs, and can only come out to play at night!

uses his feet to peel a banana!

writes long, threatening letters — and sends them to himself!

keeps a live weasel in his gym locker!

cracks walnuts between her teeth!

can fit a whole frisbee in his mouth!

considers an ax his most important school supply!

likes to growl and chase after cars!

Babysitter Puzzlers
Some Questions We've Never Been Able To Answer!

1. Why don't babysitters' boyfriends want to play six-hour games of Monopoly with you?

2. Why don't babysitters ever like to be blindfolded?

3. Why do babysitters begin to get cranky if you stay up more than five hours after your bedtime?

4. Why do babysitters have the right to tell you what you can and cannot eat — when it's your refrigerator?

5. Why do you need a babysitter up until the day you're old enough to *be* a babysitter?

Test Yourself!
Do You Know What To Say
When Disaster Strikes?

This whole book is about Sad Facts, so we thought that in this chapter we'd talk about something cheerful. Our good news is that all the terrible things that happen to you all the time are happening to your friends, too!

Do you know what to do when disaster strikes a friend? Do you know what to say? The right word at the right time can make all the difference (or maybe a little difference).

Circle the best response for each situation. Then check your score at the end of the test.

1. You're walking to school with a friend on a rainy day. A big truck roars by, splashing water all over your friend, but missing you. Your friend is totally drenched. You say:
   a) "Hahahahaha!"
   b) "That was close!"
   c) "Are you wet?"
   d) "Don't worry — they can cure most cases of pneumonia these days!"

2. During a hike in the mountains, you start horsing around with a friend and accidentally push him off a 50-foot cliff into a lake. Your friend is splashing around in the icy water, struggling to stay afloat. You say:

a) "Are you wet?"

b) "Sorry."

c) "Don't splash so much. You'll scare the ducks."

d) "Pretty good dive. Now let's see your jackknife!"

3. You and your friend are eating lunch in the cafeteria. Someone accidentally drops a huge plate of spaghetti all over your friend. Your friend is covered in tomato sauce. You say:

a) "Hahahaha!"

b) "That was close!"

c) "Hey, look out!"

d) "Okay, that was the main course. Now how about some dessert?"

4. You and your friend are at the zoo when a fierce lion escapes from its cage. The lion pounces on your friend and pins him to the ground. You say:
- a) "Uh-oh."
- b) "Down, boy."
- c) "Hey, look out!"
- d) "If you keep moving like that, how can I focus my camera?"

5. Just before a big party, your friend catches her new party dress on a nail. The dress rips all the way down the back. You say:
   a) "Feel a draft?"
   b) "Pretty sharp nail!"
   c) "Gee, that *was* a pretty dress!"
   d) "Here — I'll tear mine too, and everyone will think it's a new fad!"

6. Your girlfriend had long, silky hair down to her knees, but she got an extremely short haircut to surprise you. She's very upset because she's not sure she did the right thing. You say:
   a) "Something's different. Did you get new glasses?"
   b) "Feel a draft?"
   c) "Oh no! Oh good heavens! Oh, how awful! What did you do to your hair?!"
   d) "Now that you won't be needing it, can I borrow your hot comb?"

7. You and your friend are trying out new roller skates a few blocks from your house. You try to warn your friend about the steep hill (known as Mt. McKinley), but you are too late. Suddenly you see your friend zooming down the hill out of control at about 80 m.p.h.! You say:
   a) "Now that you won't be needing it, can I borrow your hot comb?"
   b) "Hey — slow down!"
   c) "Your shoelace is untied!"
   d) "I'll tell your mother you'll be late for dinner — and breakfast!"

Scoring: Did you know the right thing to say for each situation? Give yourself 5¼ points for each time you chose (a) or almost chose (a). Tear out five pages from this book for each time you chose (b) or wanted to choose (b) but confused it with (d). Take away 6¾ points and a week's allowance for each time you started to choose (c) but your pencil slipped and you poked yourself in the arm. Give yourself a pat on the back for each question you crossed out and wrote in your own question for. Ignore completely each time you chose (c) or (d).

85-100 Points — You are suave, sophisticated, intelligent, and well-spoken, and someday soon you are bound to stop sucking your toes at the dinner table and making everyone sick.

65-84 points — You mean to be helpful and say the right thing, but this foolish idea of yours that you are a cute and perky German shepherd puppy gets in your way. Stop barking and grow up!

40-64 points — You could do much better in choosing the correct thing to say in difficult situations, but you spend all your time taking silly tests in silly books. What a shame!

0-39 points — You are much better off as a cute and perky German shepherd puppy. Work on developing a deeper bark and stop worrying about the right thing to say — or the Sad Facts of Life!

Promises You Know You'll Never Keep

If you let me go to the movie, I'll give up television for a week.

I promise when I sleep overnight at Beth's that we won't stay up too late.

If you buy me the dog, I'll feed him every day and walk him three times a day.

I promise I won't eat too much of that chocolate cake while you're away.

I'll never hit my little brother again — even if he hits first and there's no one looking.

I promise I won't tease Susie about that stupid, silly, ugly, ridiculous haircut she got.

I'm going to take my gym clothes home to be washed next week.

I'll do my homework on Friday night so I won't have to worry about it all weekend.

I'll be home before dark!

I won't tell a single soul that you're madly in love with that new kid who moved in down the block.

If you let me off this time, I'll eat all my corn and peas next time.

This is the last shirt I'm going to buy just because it's the latest style.

When you go out tonight to the party, I'll go to bed at my regular time.

This is the 20th and last time I'm going to watch this rerun of *Happy Days*.

From now on, I'm going to resist the temptation to splash my friends at the water fountain.

I'm not going to make any more promises I can't keep.

Promises You Know Parents Will Never Keep

When you get a little older, you can decorate your own room.

If you save up enough money, you can buy a horse.

Try the lima beans. I made them a new way, and I promise you'll love them!

This is the last pair of pants you'll have to try on all year.

At the open house, we won't say anything to embarrass you in front of your teacher.

You just have to stay and talk to your grand-mother for five minutes — then you can go out-side and have fun the rest of the day.

Get your hair cut any way you want. We won't say a thing about it.

If you save up your allowance, you can spend the money on anything you want, no matter how silly it is.

The dentist isn't going to hurt you. We promise he's just going to clean your teeth.

School Supplies Puzzlers
Some Questions We've Never Been Able To Answer!

1. If a protractor is so important, how come you never see a grown-up using one?

2. Why is it impossible to close a three-ring notebook without catching your finger in one of the rings?

3. Can't they make a one-foot ruler shorter so it will fit better in your book bag?

4. Why is it impossible to open a box of those little notebook paper reinforcement rings without having them all fall out and scatter all over the floor? And why do they always stick to your thumb and not to the paper?

5. Why is it that you always leave the right supplies in your locker and bring the wrong supplies to class?

The Sad Facts of Vacation Trips

Summer comes around, and it's family vacation time. Time to pile into the car and head for a nearby lake. Could be fun, right? It also could be no fun at all. What do we mean? Well, for example, here's a diary a boy just about your age kept during his last vacation trip. We'll bet his vacation may have been just a little bit like yours. . . .

2 A.M.

Dad says he wants to get a real early start tomorrow morning, so we all went to bed early. Now, it's five hours later, and I still haven't fallen asleep. I've been awake all this time thinking about how I've got to fall asleep so we can get an early start tomorrow.

4:30 A.M.

Made a small mistake. I read the clock wrong. Thought it said 7:30. Went downstairs and woke everybody up. Boy, were they angry when they saw my little mistake. But I'm sure we'll all laugh about it in the morning. Ha ha.

5 A.M.

Heard a strange scratching noise. Couldn't figure out what it was. Turned out to be my toe scratching the wall. Silly of me. Wish I could get to sleep. I'd try counting sheep, but I don't really remember what sheep look like. Do they have long faces or short faces? I'd better try to forget about sheep, or I'll never fall asleep. Wonder if my sister Beth is sleeping. I can't wait for her to find the surprise I put into her suitcase.

9:30 A.M.

Why didn't anyone wake me? They've all been up for hours, but they let me sleep. Dad's complaining because he couldn't get back to sleep after I woke him. Beth didn't sleep all night and she's very cranky this morning. She found the rubber cockroach I put in her suitcase. Darn! She wasn't supposed to find it until we got to the motel. That was one of my best jokes, and no one thought it was funny. Mom yelled at me because I ate my cereal right from the bowl without using a spoon. I was just trying to save her a little work. Why is everyone so angry this morning?

10:15 A.M.

It took Dad a while to close the suitcases. I guess they were a little too full. Beth and I had to stand on top of them, and Dad finally was able to push them shut. He's carrying them all out to the car now. Uh-oh. My toothbrush. We forgot to pack my toothbrush. Hey, Dad — stop! My toothbrush!

10:30 A.M.

Still haven't left. I think Dad had better forget about that early start. Now there's something wrong with the luggage rack. It fell off. All the suitcases came crashing down with it. I think maybe Dad put it on wrong. He's being a pretty good sport about it. All he did was kick a hole in the side of the garage. Now he's hopping around holding his foot.

11 A.M.

Sure enough, the luggage rack is broken. Dad has to try to squeeze the suitcases into the trunk. We may have to leave my rubber raft at home — unless I can deflate it real fast. Dad says I shouldn't have blown it up until we got to the motel. He said a lot of other things I'd better not repeat. Beth cut her finger on the broken luggage rack. She was bleeding all over the clothes she was supposed to wear in the car. So now Mom has to open one of the suitcases and find her something else to wear. Only no one remembers which suitcase is Beth's. Guess Mom'll have to open them all till she finds it. I've never seen Dad with such a red face. He really looks tanned — and we haven't even started for the lake yet!

11:30 A.M.

Guess we'll be leaving pretty soon. Dad just has to figure out where to put the fishing poles, the tennis rackets, and the scuba equipment. I've been sneezing a lot this morning. Mom felt my head and she says she thinks I may have a temperature. She told Dad that maybe we should call Dr. Morgan, but he just ignored her. Dad banged his head on the lid of the trunk, and he's been pretty quiet ever since.

11:45 A.M.

I really feel okay. I wish Mom would stop feeling my forehead every five minutes. We're just about ready to leave. I volunteered to hold my rubber raft on my lap. I managed to get some of the air out of it so it shouldn't take up too much room. When Dad tried to shove it in the car, it caught on the door handle. The raft popped, just like a balloon, right in Dad's face. I told him not to worry about it. I don't really need the raft anyway — I'd rather practice my backstroke. We're going to leave now. Why is everyone in such a bad mood?

12 NOON

It really isn't like Beth to get carsick. What a shame! Especially since we were only backing down the drive. Mom said she's sure Beth will feel better as soon as we get onto the highway. Dad didn't say anything. So I guess we're off and rolling. It sure feels great to be on vacation! What's that Mom just said? She left the bathing suits at home? Yep, that's what she said. Dad's turning the car around now, and we're going back for the bathing suits.

12:30 P.M.

I'm starting to feel a little sick to my stomach. Hope I'm not catching Beth's car sickness. Mom found the bathing suits and we're on our way again. What a lucky thing she remembered! There seems to be a lot of traffic on the highway this afternoon. I guess a lot of people got an early start like us. The cars are all creeping along bumper-to-bumper. I think maybe I'm hungry. I just told Dad that I'm hungry and he tried to rip the steering wheel off the car. I wonder if that means he's hungry, too.

1:15 P.M.

We're home again. Mom couldn't remember if she locked the back door or not, so we had to come home to check. Turns out she had locked it after all. I guess the joke is on Mom! Haha! Dad closed the car door on his hand getting back into the car. He's a pretty good driver with one hand, so we're not too worried.

2:30 P.M.

Mom finally convinced Dad to stop at a restaurant along the highway for lunch. Dad agreed, since traffic was moving so slowly anyway. After lunch, Dad reached for his wallet and discovered he had left it in his other pants. All the Travelers Checks are safe and sound in one of the suitcases. Guess poor Dad's going to have to unpack the car so we can find them and pay for lunch.

4:30 P.M.

Mom bawled Beth and me out for wrestling in the back seat. But what else is there to do back here? It's so boring! We saw some dead animals on the side of the highway, but aside from that, there's nothing to look at or do. Beth has started to sing "Row Row Your Boat" again. I don't want to, but I'm going to have to hit her if she keeps it up.

5:00 P.M.

I knew the car would break down. I just had a hunch. Dad said it just overheated. There was a gas station about three miles back. He's walking there to get some water for the car. Mom and Beth and I got out of the car because it was so hot just sitting in there. I took the road map out with me for something to look at. I was trying to fold it back up — which isn't easy — and a gust of wind came up. It blew the road map away, off across a field, and I couldn't get it back. Mom says I shouldn't worry about it. She's pretty sure Dad knows the rest of the way from here. Beth just stepped in some thorny kind of plant and cut her leg. Wish Dad would get back. I'm really hungry.

7:00 P.M.

The man who towed our car to the garage was very nice. He let Beth and me ride up in the truck. Mom and Dad had a big fight on the way to the garage, but now that the car is fixed and we're on our way again, they got quiet. In fact, they've been very quiet ever since Dad said we're lost. It's really too bad about the road map. We probably wouldn't be lost if we still had it.

8:30

Mom says she knows she forgot to bring something. She doesn't know what it is. But she just has a terrible feeling that there's something she forgot to pack. Dad says we're almost to the motel. Less than an hour to go. I'm glad of that. Beth and I are getting kinda bored. We've been making funny animal noises for about half an hour, but that's pretty boring, and Dad keeps yelling for us to stop. Mom just remembered what she forgot to bring. Dad's suitcase. She had it separate, in the guest bedroom. All of Dad's clothes are in it. Thank goodness she remembered what it was she forgot. It was really driving her crazy.

10:00

Hooray! We made it! The motel is really big and it has a tiny little swimming pool in front. There seems to be a problem, though. The man at the front desk told Dad he couldn't find our reservations. He says the motel is all full and he doesn't have a room to spare. Dad's getting all red again. Dad keeps saying, "There must be some mistake" over and over. Mom says Beth and I should follow her and we'll take a look at the lake while Dad works things out. It's pretty dark back here. The lake is really big. Uh-oh. I think Beth just fell in. Mom's got her now. Yep. She fell in all right. Haha! Look at her all covered with some kind of thick scum. What a mess! Dad's calling us. He's getting back into the car. I guess we're going to drive some more. Hey, Dad — wait for us!

Haircut Puzzlers
Some Questions We've Never Been Able To Answer!

1. Why is it that no matter what you tell the haircutter, your haircut ends up three inches shorter than you wanted?

2. Why do so many people leave your barbershop with Band-Aids on the backs of their necks?

3. Can't they invent *something* so you won't have itchy little hairs down your back for days afterward?

4. Why can't the stylist ever ask first whether you want that sticky hair spray put on your hair or not?

5. Why do people always tell you you need a haircut two days after you just got one?

Say, those are good-looking sneakers you've got! But do you have the feeling as you walk into gym class that maybe you should be wearing combat boots instead? Think maybe they've assigned you to the wrong class? Well . . .

You Know You're in the Wrong Gym Class When . . .

The other kids like to use a bowling ball to play soccer!

You're required to play all sports on your hands so you won't scuff up the gym floor!

One hundred push-ups are required — before you change into your gym clothes!

The volleyball net is three stories high!

One of the older kids likes to demonstrate how to slam-dunk using one of the younger kids!

Part of the required equipment is a bullet-proof vest!

The gymnastic mats are made of brick!

The Sad Facts About Getting Presents

The shirt you just adore will be three sizes too small for you. The shirt you hate will fit perfectly.

After you spend six hours putting the model plane together, you'll discover that the most important piece is missing.

People always think it's funny to fool you by putting a tiny present in a huge box — but it isn't.

That box you think contains a video game set actually contains six pairs of socks and a pair of green suspenders.

Each year it gets harder and harder to pretend that you just love the matching sweater and cap your grandmother spends all year knitting for you.

No matter how many presents you get, you always want to play with what your younger brother got!

Your mother always makes a big deal about the wrapping paper and insists that you remove it carefully and save it. Then, when everyone leaves, she throws it away.

Don't get your hopes up that you'll be able to play with that electronic robot you just received. The batteries aren't included, and all the stores are closed because it's Sunday.

Why do the instructions for that new game you can't wait to play come in only Japanese and Italian?

Someone made a mistake at the factory, and that new jigsaw puzzle won't fit together — even if you use a sledgehammer!

If you don't pretend that you're really excited about that digital egg timer your aunt gave you, you'll really hurt her feelings.

Wasn't that thoughtful of Uncle Eddie to send that wonderful deep-sea scuba diving equipment all the way to your house in Arizona?

Your parents will not understand why you are disappointed with the beautiful portable shoe tree they gave you.

Don't get excited about the $25 your uncle gave you. Your parents are going to take it away from you "to save for your college fund."

Why do you have to read the cards first? Why can't you read the cards last?

You can't wait to show your holiday presents to your friends, and it turns out they all got exactly the same things.

Just keep smiling when your Aunt Margaret says that the candy apple she brought "is for all three of you kids to share!"

You shouldn't get too worked up about that fancy slot car set you just got. By the time your dad gets through playing with it, you will have outgrown it!

You've mixed up all the cards, and you don't remember who gave you what. Looks as if writing thank-you notes will be as much fun as always!

5 Things That Are Bound To Happen the Next Time You Try To Tell a Joke

1. You'll say, "Stop me if you've heard this one before," and someone will stop you.

2. You will get all the way through the joke, and someone will tell the punchline before you do.

3. You will get all the way through the joke and forget the punchline.

4. You will get all the way through the joke and then remember that you left out something really important in the middle.

5. You will finish telling the joke, and no one will get it.

6. You will finish telling the joke, and everyone will get it — but no one will think it's funny!

(Hey — you thought there were only supposed to be five things in this list? Well, the generous folks at Dynamite Books threw in another one — at no extra charge! Who says this book isn't a bargain!)

Preface to the Introduction

We know, we know. We promised there wouldn't be an Introduction. But now that you've read the entire book, you don't mind if we just squeeze in a teensy weensy one, do you?

We'll keep it very short. Just a few words. Promise!

After all, what's a book without an Introduction?

So, without further ado (and thanking you for your patience and understanding), here it is. . . .

A Few Introductory Words

heliotrope
lollapalooza
fiddledeedee

Practice Shelf-Hypnosis!

Cast a bright spell over your bookshelves and
turn your book collection from dull to Dynamite!
Collect the complete set of Dynamite Books.

Magic Wanda's Dynamite Magic Book
Count Morbida's Dynamite Puzzle Book
The Dynamite Party Book
The Dynamite Book of Top Secret Information
The Dynamite Monster Hall of Fame
The Dynamite Book of Bummers
The Officially Official Dynamite Club Handbook
The Dynamite Year-Round Catalog of Hot Stuff
The Dynamite People Book
Count Morbida's Fang-tastic Activity Book
Gotcha! The Dynamite Book of Sneaky Tricks,
Silly Jokes, and Harmless Pranks To Play On Your Friends
A Laugh and a Half: The Dynamite Book of Funny Stuff
The Dynamite 3-D Poster Book
The Dynamite Do-It-Yourself Pen Pal Kit
Good Vibrations: Straight Talk and Solid Advice for Kids
The Dynamite Animal Hall of Fame
The Dynamite Kids' Guide to the Movies
Dynamite's Funny Book of the Sad Facts of Life
The Dynamite Book of Ghosts and Haunted Houses
Count Morbida's Monster Quiz Book

Here to Help

POSTMAN

Hannah Phillips

Photography by Bobby Humphrey

W

FRANKLIN WATTS

LONDON·SYDNEY

Franklin Watts
First published in Great Britain in 2015 by the Watts Publishing Group

Credits
Series Editors: Hannah Phillips and Paul Humphrey
Series Designer: D. R. ink
Photographer: Bobby Humphrey
Produced for Franklin Watts by Discovery Books Ltd.
Picture credits:
All photographs are by Bobby Humphrey with the exception of: Shutterstock: page 5 (top)
Michael Rosak, page 5 (bottom) KariDesign, Page 14 Whytock, Page 15 (bottom) Evgeny
Karandaev, Page 17 Featureflash/Shutterstock.com.

Dewey number 383.4'9'41
HB ISBN: 978 1 4451 4002 5
Library ebook ISBN: 978 1 4451 4003 2

Printed in China

Franklin Watts
An imprint of
Hachette Children's Group
Part of the Watts Publishing Group
Carmelite House
50 Victoria Embankment
London EC4Y 0DZ

An Hachette UK company
www.hachette.co.uk

www.franklinwatts.co.uk

The publisher and packager would like to thank the following people for their help with
this book: Shaun Macken, the Ecclestone family, Michael Neil, Val Bodden and all the
staff at Telford sorting office.